Bakery

Bakery

Text: Susan Pepper

Photography: Chris Fairclough

Franklin Watts

LONDON/NEW YORK/SYDNEY/TORONTO

Your guide

Herb Schwarz is the Production Manager of the Austral bakery in Melbourne, Australia. He has been a baker for 38 years and has worked for the Home Pride company for the past 20 years.

Contents

Franklin Watts Limited
12a Golden Square
London W1R 4BA
Copyright © 1984 Franklin
Watts Limited
ISBN: 0 86313 110 7
Phototypeset by Tradespools Limited,
Frome, Somerset
Printed in Singapore

Text Editor: Brenda Williams
Educational Consultant: Henry Pluckrose
Design: Peter Benoist
Illustrator: Tony Payne
The publishers, author and photographer would
like to thank Austral Bakeries for their help in the
preparation of this book. They are especially
grateful to Bernie Day and David Hennessy,
and to all those working at the bakery.

Inside a bakery

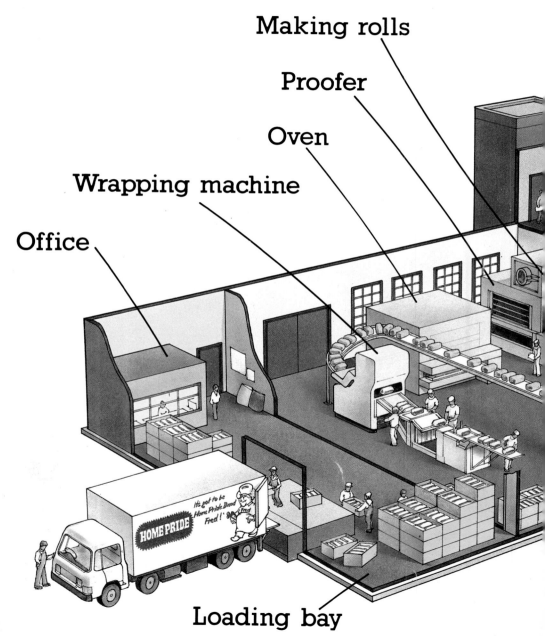

Making rolls

Proofer

Oven

Wrapping machine

Office

HOME PRIDE

It's got to be Home Pride Bread Fred! Fred

Loading bay

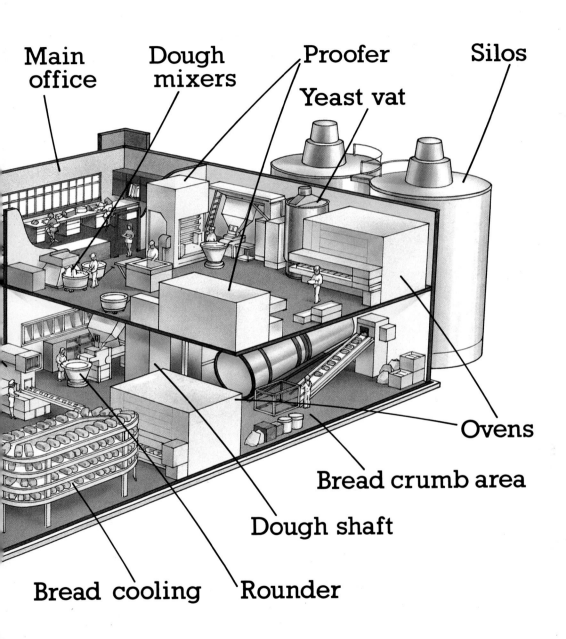

Main office

Dough mixers

Proofer

Yeast vat

Silos

Ovens

Bread crumb area

Dough shaft

Bread cooling

Rounder

9

Bread

Bakeries make all sorts of bread. This bakery is at work day and night making white loaves, brown wholemeal bread and fruit loaves. It also makes buns, rolls and breadsticks. Sometimes the bakery has visitors. They see how bread is made and enjoy a hamburger bun!

Flour arrives at the bakery
twice a day. It comes in huge
trucks which can carry loads
of 22 tonnes. The flour is stored
in silos outside the building.
Other ingredients are also
delivered daily.

Bakers

Few people handle the bread in a bakery. It is mostly made by machines, which are controlled from this panel. It is hot work in the bakery and so cool clothing is worn. Some people also wear ear pads to keep out the noise.

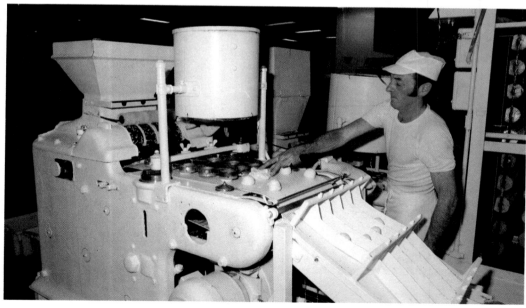

The ingredients

The heavy bags of ingredients are moved around on trolleys. Bread has four main ingredients. These are flour, yeast, salt and water. Some loaves are also made with milk, fat, sultanas and various spices.

Making the dough

The baker is ready to make a batch of loaves. He decides how much of each ingredient is needed. The ingredients must be weighed carefully or the dough will not rise. One mixture will make over 400 large loaves.

14

The baker puts all the dry
ingredients into a big metal
bowl. Warm water is added
slowly. Then the bowl is turned
as a dough hook mixes the
ingredients. The dough
becomes soft and springy
after four minutes.

The divider

When the dough is ready it is tipped into the divider. Here it is quickly cut into small pieces. These are weighed and then rolled into balls by the rounder. Each piece of dough will become a loaf. It must be the correct weight.

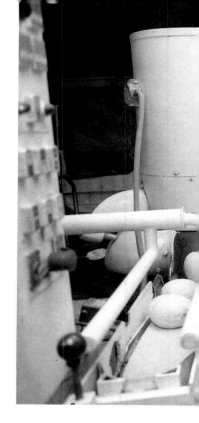

The divider cuts smaller pieces of dough for rolls, buns and breadsticks. The rounding machine shapes these into smooth balls. A rounding machine for rolls can shape 16 balls at a time. Fancy rolls are shaped by hand.

Baking tins

Baking tins are made ready in another part of the building. Cooking oil is squirted into the tins to stop the dough from sticking. The oil also gives a crisp crust to the cooked loaf.

18

A moulder then shapes each ball of dough into a loaf. The dough is dropped into a tin and left in a warm place to rise. This is called proving. The yeast in the dough forms tiny bubbles and so makes the mixture grow.

The oven

Now the dough is ready for the oven. A lid is put on each tin before it goes inside. The bread moves on a conveyor belt. It starts at the top of the oven and is cooked by the time it reaches the bottom. This takes 30 minutes. Rolls go into an oven on trays.

Dough comes out of the oven as loaves and rolls. A magnet pulls off the tin lids and the bread is sucked out. It is left to cool for an hour and a half. The tins and lids are also left to cool before being used again.

Wrapping and packing

Loaves are checked by a quality controller. Most bread is then sliced by machine and wrapped in a plastic bag. The bag is blown open by a gust of air and then pulled over the loaf. The end is tied. Some of the rolls are left unwrapped.

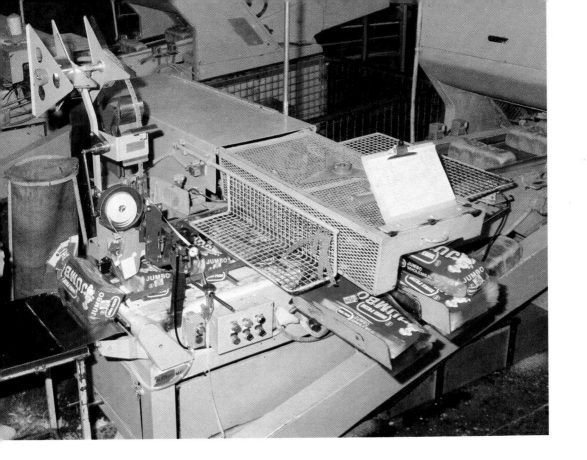

Wrapped loaves are packed into plastic trays ready for the shops and supermarkets. Delivery vans leave the bakery at 3.00 a.m. The bread will reach the shops before they open for the day.

23

Breadcrumbs

Any bread which the shops do not sell is sent back to the bakery to be made into breadcrumbs. The loaf is unwrapped and put on a conveyor belt. It goes through a machine which breaks it up finely. Then the crumbs are dried in a heated drum and packed into large bags.

Apprentices

Only qualified bakers are able to mix the dough. Bakers' apprentices learn about breadmaking at college. Here they look at bread made by hand and by machine. Machines cannot make bread into fancy shapes.

Maintenance

Baking will stop if a machine breaks down. So the machines are checked every morning. One or two may need attention while they are working. Parts for some machines are made at the bakery.

All machines are carefully
cleaned at the end of the day.
Sticky dough is scraped from
the mixing bowls and the floor
is swept once more. Places
where food is made must be
kept as clean as possible.

Facts and figures

The bakery shown in this book makes over a million loaves and bread rolls each week.

Over 350 tonnes of flour are used by the bakery every week. Over 15,000 tonnes of flour are used each year.

More than 200 people work at the bakery.

The temperature in the oven is 240°C (460°F). In the proving room the temperature is 40°C (104°F).

Bread is made from wheat or rye. Some bread includes other grains such as corn, barley and millet. Some bread contains soya flour.

The longest loaf made in one piece was 141 metres (154 yards) long. It was made in California in 1975.

People in Britain eat about 10 million large loaves of bread a day. This is about 29,200 million kilograms of bread a year (6387.5 million lbs).

77% of bread sold in Britain is white, 13% brown and wholemeal and the remaining 10% is speciality breads such as malt and milk loaves.

Two-thirds of the bread eaten in Britain is sliced, and one-third unsliced.

People in Britain get 15% of the total protein they need from the bread they eat.

Bread has been eaten for at least 7,500 years. In Britain, records relating to the price of bread go back as far as the reign of King John (1199–1216).

Glossary

Apprentice A person who is learning a trade. Some apprentices work by day and study at college by night.

Bakery A place where bread is cooked in an oven.

Breadsticks Long, thin sticks of crunchy bread.

Dough The raw, spongy mixture which becomes bread when it is cooked.

Dough hook A large metal hook, part of the machine which mixes the dough.

Fruit loaves Bread which has currants, sultanas or raisins added. It is sweeter than ordinary bread.

Ingredients The various materials that are mixed together to make a particular food.

Magnet A piece of metal which has been specially treated so that it attracts other metals to it.

Proving The name given to the time when the yeast is working and the dough grows in size.

Recipe A list of ingredients and the instructions for mixing and cooking them.

Silo A large metal tank used for storing grain or flour.

Sultana A small seedless raisin, or dried grape.

Wholemeal Flour with the bran left in it. Bran is the skin of the grain. White flour has no bran.

Yeast The ingredient which makes dough rise. It is a plant and is killed by the heat of the oven.

Index